William Shakespeare's
ROMEO & JULIET

Adapted by Gareth Jones

Prologue

{This can be read by any combination of cast or teachers in any way you wish. The chorus, as a football crowd, can be chanting at different volumes throughout the piece. A drum would be a useful instrument to create atmosphere and tension}.

Far or Near. Then or Now.
 Our story is one oft told and heard.
A story of Love.
A story of Friendship which knows no bounds.
A story of Hatred which destroys the ones we love.

This is the story of Romeo and Juliet,
Of Tony and Maria,
And now,
Of {Insert Names}.

Act 1

It is a time of darkness.

The town is riven by dissension.

Two families are locked in anger. It is an historic discord between…..

Chorus / Two households both alike in dignity,
In fair Verona where we lay our scene,
From ancient grudge break to new mutiny.
Where civil blood makes civil hands unclean.
From forth the fatal loins of these two foes
A pair of star crossed lovers take their life;
Whose misadventured piteous overthrows
Doth with their death bury their parents' strife.
The fearful passage of their death marked love,
And the continuance of their parents' rage,
Which, but for their children's end, nought could remove,

Is now the shortened traffic of our stage;

To which if you with patient ears attend,

What here shall miss, our toil shall strive to mend.

Narrator/s / And so our tale begins. Two servants of the Capulets were strolling in the city streets and looking for a fight with their ancient enemies, the Montagues!

{There is a chorus either side of the stage. They are both dressed in different football colours and chanting as football supporters do}.

Chorus 1 / Capulet, Capulet, Capulet etc.

Chorus 2 / Montague, Montague, Montague etc.

Gregory / Draw thy tool, here comes of the house of Montagues.

Sampson / My naked weapon is out. Quarrel, I will back thee.

Gregory / I will frown as they pass by and let them take it as they list.

Sampson / Nay, as they dare. I will bite my thumb at them, which is disgrace to them if they bare it.

Abraham / Do you bite your thumb at us sir?

Sampson / I do bite my thumb sir.

Abraham / Do you bite your thumb at us sir?

Sampson / No sir, I do not bite my thumb at you sir, but I bite my thumb sir!

Gregory / Do you quarrel sir?

Abraham / Quarrel sir? No sir!

{Chorus 1 & 2 now chant more loudly and might even throw things at each other}.

Narrator / And so it went on. Each day the streets of Verona were disturbed by the arguments and taunts of the rival Houses. The Duke was not a happy man.

Duke / I am not a happy man!

Narrator / In fact, he was so unhappy that he made a very powerful and dangerous decision!

Duke / Rebellious subjects, enemies of peace,
Profaners of this neighbour-stained steel-
Will they not hear? What ho! You men, you beasts,
that quench the fire of your pernicious rage
with purple fountains issuing from your veins,
On pain of torture, from these bloody hands
Throw your mistempered weapons to the ground,
And hear the sentence of your moved Prince!

If ever you disturb our streets again,
Your lives shall pay the forfiet of the peace.

Narrator / And so the scene was set for the tragedy to take place. Two families at war,

{Echoes of the chanting}

A Duke determined to keep the peace in gentle Verona, and two youngsters about to fall into a forbidden love! Ironic too that they meet at a ball to make the peace. First Juliet's Father welcomes his guests.

Capulet / Welcome gentlemen. Lady's that have their toes unplagued with corns will walk a bout with you. You are welcome, gentlemen. Come musicians play.
A hall, a hall, give room and foot it girls.

Narrator / And whilst the ladies danced and the fathers talked Romeo first set eyes on Juliet.

Romeo / {To a servingman} What ladies that which doth enrich the hand of yonder knight?

Servingman / I know not Sir.

Romeo / O she doth teach the torches to burn bright.
It seems she hangs upon the cheek of night
Like a rich jewel on an Ethiops ear;
Beauty too rich for use, for earth to dear.
Did my heart love till now? Forswear it sight,
For ne'er I saw true beauty till this night.

Narrator / But now, Tybalt, of the house of Capulet, recognises Romeo as an enemy and becomes very angry.

Tybalt / This by his voice should be a Montague.
Fetch me my rapier, boy. What dares the slave

Come hither, covered with an antic face,
To fleer and scorn at our solemnity?
Now by the stock and honour of my kin,
To strike him dead I hold not as a sin!

Narrator / But Capulet will brook no insult to his guests.

Capulet / Content thee gentle coz, let him alone.
A bears him like a portly gentleman;
And to say truth, Verona brags of him
To be a virtuous and well governed youth.
It is my will, the which if thou respect,
Show a fair presence, and put off these frowns,
An ill-beseeming semblance for a feast.

Narrator / They argue more before Tybalt agrees then to withdraw, but with a threat on his lips.

Tybalt / Patience perforce with wilful choler meeting
Makes my flesh tremble in their different greeting.

I will withdraw, but this intrusion shall,
Now seeming sweet, convert to bitterest gall!

{The chorus volume now rises with the chanting of the family names}.

Narrator / With Tybalt gone Romeo and Juliet are now able to talk for the first time.

Romeo / {To Juliet} If I profane with my unworthiest hand this holy shrine, the gentle sin is this,
My lips to blushing pilgrims ready stand
To smooth that rough touch with a tender kiss.

Juliet / Good pilgrim, you do wrong your hand too much, which mannerly devotion shows in this;
For saints have hands that pilgrims hands do touch,
And palm to palm is holy palmers' kiss.

Narrator / And so the die is cast. Our two young lovers are hopelessly head over heals. Only to discover that each is the child of the others worst enemy.

Romeo / Is she a Capulet?
Dear account, my life is my foes debt.

Nurse / His name is Romeo, and a Montague,
The only son of your great enemy.

Juliet / My only love sprung from my only hate,
Too early seen unknown and known too late!
Prodigious birth of love it is to me,
That I must love a loathed enemy.

Act Two

{Chorus chanting opens up the Act, and then they say}

Chorus / Now Romeo is beloved and loves again,
Alike bewitched by the charm of look;
{But} being held a foe, he may not have access
To breathe such vows as lovers use to swear;
And she as much in love, her means much less
To meet her new beloved anywhere.

Narrator / Barred from seeing each other our young lovers are reduced to secret plans to keep their love alive. Romeo escapes his friends and creeps in to the garden of the house of Capulet where he sees Juliet upon her balcony.

Romeo / But soft, what light from yonder window breaks?

It is the east, and Juliet is the sun.

Arise fair sun and kill the envious moon,

Who is already sick and pale with grief

That thou her maid art far more fair than she.

Juliet / O Romeo, Romeo, wherefore art thou Romeo?

Deny thy father and refuse thy name.

Be some other name.

What's in a name? That which we call a rose

By any other word would smell as sweet.

Narrator / They talk of love and the danger that they are in. But the danger is not important to them, only their love matters. Juliet asks him if he intends to marry her and when he says yes she promises to send a faithful messenger the following day to discover when and where. Then they part.

Juliet / Good night, good night. Parting is such sweet sorrow.

Romeo / Sleep dwell upon thine eyes, peace in thy breast.

Would I were sleep and peace so sweet to rest!

{They both exit}

Narrator / Romeo now finds his friend and advisor Friar Lawrence. A holy man well known for his knowledge of plants, herbs and potions.

F. Lawrence / Within the infant rind of this weak flower poison hath residence, and medicine power; For this being smelt with that part cheers each part; Being tasted, stays all senses of the heart.

{Enter Romeo}

Romeo / Good morrow Father.

F. Lawrence / What early tongue so sweet saluteth me?
Young son, it argues a distempered head
So soon to bid good morrow to thy bed.
Or if not so, then here I hit it right,
Our Romeo hath not been in bed tonight!

Romeo / That last is true; the sweeter rest was mine.

F. Lawrence / But where hast though been then?

Romeo / I have been feasting with mine enemy.

F. Lawrence / Be plain good son and homely in thy drift.

Romeo / Then plainly know my hearts true love is set on the fair daughter of rich Capulet.
As mine on hers, so hers is set on mine!

F. Lawrence / Now come, young lover, come with

me.

In this respect I'll thy assistant be;

For this alliance may so happy prove,

To turn your households rancour to pure love.

Narrator / And so the Friar agrees to help in the hope that the love between Romeo and Juliet could stop the war between the families.

{They exit as Mercutio and Benvolio enter}

Mercutio / Where the devil could this Romeo be? Came he not home tonight?

Benvolio / Not to his father's, and Tybalt, the kinsman to old Capulets, hath sent a letter to his father's house.

Mercutio / A challenge, on my life.

Benvolio / Romeo will answer it.

Mercutio / Alas poor Romeo, he is already dead.

Benvolio / Why? What is Tybalt?

Mercutio / More than Prince of Cats!

Narrator / And so it seems that Tybalt, a mighty warrior has challenged Romeo to a duel which Romeo is sure to lose! But fate now intervenes in the form of Mercutio.

Benvolio / By my head, here come the Capulets.

Mercutio / By my heel, I care not.

Tybalt / Gentlemen, a word with one of you.

Mercutio / Make it a word and a blow.

Tybalt / Mercutio, though consorts with Romeo.

Mercutio / Consorts? Does though make us minstrels? Zounds! Consorts!

{Enter Romeo}

Tybalt / Well peace be with you, here comes my man.
Romeo! Thou art a villain.

Romeo / Villain am I none. Therefore farewell. I se thou knowest me not.

Tybalt / Boy! This shall not excuse the injuries that though has done me! therefore turn and draw!

Mercutio / Tybalt! You Rat catcher.

Tybalt / I am for you.

Romeo / Gentle Mercutio, put up thy rapier.

{A fight begins during which Mercutio is run through and Tybalt leaves}.

Mercutio / I am hurt. A plague on both your houses.

{He is helped off by Benvolio}.

Romeo / This gentleman, the Prince's near ally, My very friend, hath got his mortal hurt in my behalf!

{Benvolio re-enters}.

Benvolio / O Romeo, Romeo, brave Mercutio is dead.

{Tybalt now re-enters}.

Romeo / Now Tybalt take the villain back again
      That late thou gavest me, for Mercutio's soul

Is but a little way above our heads,
Staying for thine to keep him company.

Tybalt / Thou wretched boy, shalt with him hence.

{They fight and Tybalt is slain}.

Benvolio / Romeo, away, be gone. The Prince will doom thee death if thou art taken.

{Romeo exits}.

Prince / Benvolio, who began this bloody fray?

Benvolio / Tybalt, here slain, whom Romeos hand did slay.

L. Capulet / I beg for justice, which thou, Prince must give.
Romeo slew Tybalt. Romeo must not live.

Prince / Hold! For that offense immediately we do exhile him hence. Let Romeo hence in haste,
Else when he's found, that hour is his last.
Bear hence this body and attend our will.
Mercy but murders, pardoning those that kill.

{They all exit, or maybe freeze}

Narrator / And so Romeo is banished, but he does not leave at once but rather waits in the cell of Friar Lawrence for news of his beloved Juliet. Juliet though is about to discover that Romeo, her Husband, has killed Tybalt, her cousin. Her loves and loyalties are mightily confused.

Nurse / O courteous Tybalt, honest gentleman,
That I should ever live to see you dead!

Juliet/ What storm is this that blows so contrary?
    Is Romeo slaughtered? And is Tybalt dead?
    For who is living, if these two are dead?

Nurse / Tybalt is gone, and Romeo banished. Romeo that killed him, he is banished.

Juliet / My husband lives that Tybalt would have slain, and Tybalt's dead, that would have slain my husband.

Narrator / Juliet, overcome with grief, retires to her chamber. The Nurse goes to the cell of Friar Lawrence in search of Romeo. Romeo wants to die, as does Juliet, but they are both restrained. Friar Lawrence and the Nurse advise against rashness but Romeo and Juliet insist on meeting. Meanwhile Paris, another Noble, is also asking for the hand of Juliet. Her parents agree that they will be married, the next Thursday! Romeo and Juliet do not yet know this has happened.

Juliet / Wilt thou be gone? It is not yet near day.

Romeo / I must be gone and live, or stay and die.

Nurse / Madam, your lady Mother is coming to your chamber.

Juliet / Then window let light in, and let life out.

Romeo / Farewell!

Juliet / O think'st that we shall ever meet again?
Romeo / I doubt it not! And trust my love in my eye so do you!

{He exits and Lady Capulet enters}.

Narrator / Juliet does not take the news well and a huge row develops between Juliet and her parents. She refuses to marry the man of their choice and so they reject her. When they have gone, she sends the Nurse after them to say that she has gone to Friar Lawrence's to do penance for her sins, but really, she has other plans. Once there she meets Paris and rejects him to his face. He leaves and she plots with the Friar. He has an idea.

Friar / I do spy a kind of hope,
If, rather than to marry County Paris,
thou hast the strength of will to slay thyself,
Then it is likely thou wilt undertake a thing like
death, and if thou darest, I'll give thee remedy.

Juliet / O bid me leap, rather than marry Paris,
    From off the battlements of any tower!

F. Lawrence / Hold then, go home, be merry, give consent to marry Paris. Tomorrow night look that thou lie alone,
Take though this vial, being then in bed,
And this distilling liquor drink thou off;
Each part, deprived of supple government,
Shall stiff and stark appear like death.
Thou shalt continue two and forty hours,

And then awake as from a pleasant sleep.
Thou shalt be bourne {whilst sleeping} to that same ancient vault, where all the Capulets lie.
Shall Romeo by my letters know our drift,
And hither shall he come, that very night
Shall Romeo bear the hence to Mantua.

{As the following speech is made Juliet is carried in procession and laid on her tomb at the front of the stage}.

Narrator / And so the plan was made. Juliet was to take a potion which made her look as if she was dead. The Friar was to write to Romeo so that he would go to her tomb as she revived and they would both then escape to Mantua. The first part of the plan worked all too well but the second not at all. The Friars messenger was sealed into a plague house and the only message Romeo received told of the death of his beloved Juliet. Armed with a deadly poison he resolved to go to her tomb outside the walls of ancient Verona to join her in paradise. The Friar realises the plan has failed and rushes also to the tomb to rescue Juliet so that he can hide her until Romeo can be reached, not knowing that the fatal knowledge has already been received. Paris is also there to say his own farewells.

Paris / Sweet flower, with flowers thy bridal bed I strew. O woe, thy canopy is dust and stones. {There is a whistle}, the boy gives warning something doth approach. What, with a torch? Muffle me night awhile. {He hides}.

Romeo / Why I do descend into this bed of death,
Is partly to behold my ladies face;
But chiefly to take from her dead finger
A precious ring, a ring that I must use in dear employment.

Narrator / Paris does not know of Romeo's love and assumes that he has come to do harm.

Paris / This is that banished Montague, and here is come to do some villainous shame to the dead bodies. I will apprehend him! Condemned villain, I do apprehend thee.
Obey and go with me, for thou must die!

Romeo / I must indeed, and therefore came I hither.
    Good gentle youth, stay not, be gone, live.

Paris / I do defy thy conjuration.

Romeo / The have at thee!

Narrator / They fight above the grave and Paris is mortally wounded.

Paris / O I am slain. If thou be merciful,
    Open the tomb, lay me with Juliet.

Romeo / In faith I will, noble county Paris,

I'll bury thee in a triumphant grave.

Forgive me. Ah, dear Juliet

Why art thou so fair. I will stay with thee,

And never from this palace of dim night depart again.

Come bitter conduct, come unsavoury guide.

Thou desperate pilot, now at once run on

The dashing rocks thy sea-sick weary bark.

Here's to my love! {drinks} O true apothecary!

Thy drugs are quick. Thus, with a kiss I die.

Narrator / The Friar now arrives to find Romeo and Paris dead and Juliet awaking. She will not leave with noise.

Juliet / What's here? A cup closed in my true love's hand?

Poison I see hath been his timeless end.

Yea, noise? Then I'll be brief. O happy dagger!

{She stabs herself and dies}.

Narrator / By now the word has spread. The page of Paris has fetched the guard and now all the parents and the Prince arrive to witness the sorry scene. The Friar is called upon to explain the tragedy and he does. When his tale is done the Prince turns to Montague and Capulet, who first make their peace in the midst of their grief.

Capulet / O brother Montague give me thy hand. This is my daughter's jointure, for no more can I demand.

Montague / But I can give thee more.
    For I will raise her statue in pure gold,
    That whiles Verona by that name is known,
    There shall no figure at such rate be set
    As that of true and faithful Juliet.

Capulet / As rich shall Romeo by his lady lie,
    Poor sacrifices of our enmity.

Prince / A glooming peace this morning with it brings; The sun for sorrow will not show his head. Go hence to have more talk of these sad things; Some shall be pardoned, and some punished.

Everyone still standing /
For never was a story of more woe
Than this of Juliet and her Romeo.

THE END

All rights, including adaption for Film, TV, Stage or any form of internet screening, are strictly reserved. No part of this publication may be reproduced, stored in a retrieval system, or transmitted at any times by any means electronic, mechanical, photocopying, recording or otherwise without the prior permission of the copyright holder.
©Gareth Jones 2015 {revised November 2019}

Also by Gareth Jones

Non-Fiction

On This Day for Teachers

Saving the Planet, one step at a time {as "Plays in the Rain"}

Dealer's Choice, The Home Poker Game Handbook

Mametz Wood, Three Stories of Wales {First published by Bretwalda}

Outstanding School Trip Leadership

Top Teacher Tips for Outstanding Behaviour for Learning {as Gethin James}

Cheeky Elf Solutions for Busy Parents

A Short Report on the Planet known locally as Earth {as Abel Star}

Make Your Own Teepee {First published by Bretwalda}

Travelling with Children {First published by Bretwalda. Now in its second edition and fully illustrated}

Identifying Gifted and Talented Children, and what to do next

Outstanding Transition, A Teacher's Guide

An Unofficial set of revision notes for the Edexcel GCSE, History B, American West

An Unofficial set of revision notes for the Edexcel GCSE, History B, Medicine Unit

The Big Activity Book for KS3 Drama {published by ZigZag}

The Drama Handbook KS2 {this is an age adapted version of the above. They should not be bought together}

Fiction

Heart Song, A Novel

Short Stories {also fiction}

The Christmas Owls {Based on an idea by Millie Carzana}

The Pheasant that Refused to Fly {includes "The Cave." Winner of the 2018 Hailsham Arts Festival

Short Story Competition}

The Unicorns of Moons Hill and the Broken Heart {Based on an idea by Millie Carzana}

An Owl called Moonlight and The Midnight Tree {Based on an idea by Millie Carzana}

Plays

Georgina and the Dragon {First published by Schoolplay}

Jason and the Astronauts {Also first published by Schoolplay}

Dr Milo's Experiment

The Space Pirate Panto

Cinderella and the Raiders of the Lost Slipper {includes "Goldilocks," the full story}

William Tell, The Panto

Undefinable

Short Stories and Plot Outlines that would make GREAT FILMS, Mr Steven Spielberg, Sir

Quick Comedy Sketches for Young Comedians {as performed
at "The Paragon Spectacular, White Rock Theatre, Hastings}

The Quiz That Keeps on Giving. A Charity Fund Raiser

The Amazing Adventures of Edwina Elf

JPR Williams X-Rayed my Head

Printed in Poland
by Amazon Fulfillment
Poland Sp. z o.o., Wrocław